D1498910

RIVER
ADVENTURES
MISSISSIPPI
RIVER

A⁺
Smart Apple Media

Published by Smart Apple Media
P.O. Box 3263, Mankato, Minnesota 56002
www.smartapplemedia.com

Published by arrangement with the Watts Publishing Group
LTD, London.

Library of Congress Cataloging-in-Publication Data

Manning, Paul, 1954-
 The Mississippi River / Paul Manning.
     p. cm. -- (River adventures)
 Includes index.
 Summary: "Readers will travel through the heartland of
America to the bayous of Louisiana in this journey down the
Mississippi River. Learn about cities, the tributaries, and the
system of locks and dams on the mighty Mississippi River"--
Provided by publisher.
 ISBN 978-1-59920-916-6 (library binding)
 1. Mississippi River--Juvenile literature. 2. Mississippi River
Valley--Juvenile literature. I. Title.
 F351.M33 2015
 977--dc23
                            2012035418

ISBN: 978-1-59920-916-6   (library binding)
ISBN: 978-1-62588-586-9   (eBook)

Design, editing, picture research by Paul Manning

Printed in the United States by CG Book Printers
North Mankato, Minnesota

PO 1732
3-2015

9 8 7 6 5 4 3 2 1

Note to Teachers and Parents

Every effort has been made to ensure that the websites
listed on page 32 are suitable for children, that they are of
the highest educational value, and that they contain no
inappropriate or offensive material. However, because of the
nature of the Internet, it is impossible to guarantee that
the content of these sites will not be altered. We strongly
recommend that Internet access is supervised by
a responsible adult.

Key to images

Top cover image: The skyline of Minneapolis
Main cover image: Cargo ships on the Mississippi
Previous page: A North American bald eagle
This page: Panorama of St. Anthony Falls, Minneapolis

Picture Credits

CONTENTS

A Mississippi Journey

The Mississippi River flows 2,300 miles (3,700 km) from Minnesota in the northern United States to the Gulf of Mexico. It is not the longest U.S. river (the Missouri is longer), but it is the most important route for ships and transport. You will follow the river from its **source** to the sea.

A Mighty River

The Mississippi is like the United States itself: vast, powerful, and always changing. The river has played a vital part in the country's history. People have used it for transportation, farming, and industry since early times. It is one of the busiest working rivers in the world, carrying boats loaded with goods and raw materials from all over the North American continent.

▼ *The Mississippi* **floodplain** *contains the richest farmland in the United States.*

Map labels:

SASKATCHEWAN
CANADA
NORTH DAKOTA
Lake Itasca
MONTANA
MINNESOTA
MISSOURI RIVER
Coon Rapids
Minneapolis · St. Paul
WISCONSIN
MISSISSIPPI RIVER
WYOMING
SOUTH DAKOTA
MISSOURI RIVER
NEBRASKA
Des Moines
Chicago
ROCKY MOUNTAINS
GREAT PLAINS
Omaha
IOWA
ILLINOIS
COLORADO
Kansas City
Springfield
INDIANA
KANSAS
St. Louis
MISSOURI
KENTUCKY
UNITED STATES
OKLAHOMA
ARKANSAS
TENNESSEE
Oklahoma City
MISSISSIPPI RIVER
Memphis
TEXAS
ALABAMA
GEORGIA
MISSISSIPPI
Baton Rouge
LOUISIANA
New Orleans
MEXICO
Gulf of Mexico

N W E S

Birth of a River

The Mississippi River was formed during the last ice age, 10,000–12,000 years ago. At that time, most of Earth was covered with **glaciers**. When the ice melted, water flowed across the land, forming the Mississippi **channel**. The name "Mississippi" comes from Native American words meaning "Big River."

▼ This bald eagle lives by catching fish in the Mississippi. It uses its powerful **talons** to snatch fish from the river.

Mississippi Wildlife

The Mississippi is home to about 240 species of fish and 50 different **mammals**. Moose and eagles live along the upper reaches of the river. The bald eagle is the national symbol of the United States and is a protected species. Alligators and muskrats make their homes in the lower Mississippi.

The River Source

CANADA

Lake Itasca

UNITED STATES

MINNESOTA

Mississippi River

Minneapolis

St. Paul

YOU ARE HERE

The place where a river begins is called its **source**. The source of the Mississippi is Lake Itasca in northern Minnesota. The river starts life as a small, clear stream flowing out of the lake.

▼ At Lake Itasca in Minnesota, a wooden post and a line of stepping stones mark the spot where the Mississippi begins.

Lake Itasca is shallow and surrounded by pine forests. Many tourists come here to see where the Mississippi begins.

As the stream heads south, it twists and turns through lakes and marshes and over waterfalls. The area has few towns or cities, but it is popular with tourists for walking, camping, and fishing. Special lands, called **reservations**, are set aside for Native American groups such as the Ojibwe, who live close to the river's source.

▶ Minnesota has nearly 12,000 lakes that are greater than 10 acres (4 ha). They are popular for canoeing and fishing.

Hunter-gatherers

Roughly 7,000–8,000 years ago, tribes such as the Ojibwe hunted wild animals for food by the river. These early people lay in wait for bison, deer, and moose at the water's edge and killed them with stone-tipped spears.

Later, other Native American groups arrived in the region. They built larger, more permanent settlements and made a variety of stone, wood, and bone tools. The ancient burial mounds they left behind can still be seen at Itasca's Indian Cemetery.

The Mound Builders

Long ago, America's first farming peoples lived alongside the Mississippi. Because of the earthen mounds they left behind, they are sometimes known as the mound builders. Some mounds supported temples. Others were used as burial sites. Mounds continued to be built until as late as the sixteenth century.

▶ Burial mounds dating back to prehistoric times can be found throughout the Mississippi valley.

YOU ARE HERE

The Upper River

You are now traveling the Upper Mississippi. This reaches from the source at Lake Itasca to where the Mississippi River meets the Missouri River north of St. Louis.

▼ The Mississippi is a vital transport route for industry. Fleets of flat-bottomed boats called barges carry all kinds of goods. These include flour, corn, coal, iron, steel, and timber.

The River Highway

On the Mississippi, the channel used by boats is at least 9 feet (2.7 m) deep throughout its length. To keep it open, **sediment** has to be cleared from the riverbed by special boats called **dredgers**. Between Lake Itasca and St. Louis, a system of dams is also used to make sure there is always enough water in the channel for boats.

◀ The huge prairie that stretches across the Upper Mississippi is known as America's "corn belt." As well as corn, soybean production is an important crop here.

Clear Water

The upper river is mostly clear of **silt**. Its color does not change until it meets the muddy, red waters of the Missouri to the south. It flows through rolling hills, marshland, and flat grassland called **prairie**. The soils are **fertile**, and farmers grow corn and wheat beside the river. Forests of pine, maple, oak, and hickory also grow here.

River Wildlife

The Upper Mississippi is home to many wild animals. Black bears wait on the banks to catch fish in the river. Deer and beavers search for food nearby. Millions of birds **migrate** and use the river on their journeys between Canada and the United States. Their migration route is called the Mississippi Flyway.

▶ Black bears are the most common bears in North America. They grow to about 6 feet (1.8 m) tall and weigh 200–600 pounds (90–270 kg).

YOU ARE HERE

Dams and Locks

At Coon Rapids, named for the **raccoons** once found there, you stop to explore one of the many dams on the Upper Mississippi.

Controlling the River

Dams hold back the water and form a deeper channel so that boats can travel up and down the river. The dams also allow water to be stored in **reservoirs**. This water can then be used for **irrigating** fields or released back into the river if the water level is low. The first dams were built on the Upper Mississippi in the 1880s. Later, more dams were built between Minneapolis and St. Louis.

▼ Coon Rapids Dam was originally built to provide **hydroelectric** power for homes and factories. Today, the dam reservoir is mainly used for recreation.

◀ A barge enters a lock chamber on the Mississippi. When the lock gates are shut, the water level inside the chamber can be raised or lowered.

Locks

South of Minneapolis, locks were built to allow barges to bypass dams and travel all the way up and down the river. The locks work like lifts, raising or lowering the water level. This allows boats to transfer safely to the next stretch of river.

Beside the locks, there are also pools and reservoirs. These are widely used for recreation. Each year, millions of people visit the pools to camp, picnic, go boating, or watch wildlife.

What is a wing dam?

A wing dam is a barrier that only extends partway into a river. Its job is to force water into a fast-moving center channel and to stop sediment from building up on the riverbed. The Mississippi has thousands of wing dams. Many are below the surface of the water and sometimes can be a **hazard** for boats.

▶ Kayakers avoid a wing dam on a man-made section of the riverbed.

CANADA

Lake Itasca

UNITED STATES

MINNESOTA

Minneapolis

Mississippi River

St. Paul

YOU ARE HERE

The Twin Cities

Minneapolis, together with its twin city, St. Paul, is home to almost 3 million people. The two cities border each other. Their central downtown districts are about 10 miles (16 km) apart.

A Mill Town

▼ The St. Anthony Falls in Minneapolis are the only natural waterfalls on the river.

The city of Minneapolis grew up just north of where the Mississippi joins the Minnesota River. In the early days, water from the St. Anthony Falls provided energy for local industries. The river also provided the transport route for bringing raw materials into the city and taking finished goods out.

◄ This photo of St. Paul, Minnesota, was taken in winter. At that time of year, parts of the river sometimes freeze over completely.

Thanks to the river and the railways, Minneapolis quickly grew into a thriving mill town. Huge farms in the north-west grew wheat. The **harvests** were transported into the city by hundreds of rail wagons.

A Financial Center

Today, most of the city's wealth comes from financial services. However, in the Mill City Museum and the restored waterfront area, you can still see reminders of the days when Minneapolis was a busy industrial center.

Water Power

Above St. Anthony Falls, water was **diverted** from the Mississippi into a system of canals and used to turn wooden **waterwheels**. These provided the energy for sawmills, flour mills, and paper mills. Sometimes, so much water was diverted from the river that St. Anthony Falls ran dry!

▶ The **stern wheel** of a Mississippi steamboat is on display outside the Mill City Museum in Minneapolis.

13

The Working River

YOU ARE HERE

Beyond Minneapolis, the Mississippi widens. Between here and St. Louis, it is joined by the Minnesota, Wisconsin, Illinois, and Missouri Rivers. Together, they form one of the world's great transport networks.

▼ A single tugboat (right of picture) steers a fleet of more than 50 barges on the river north of St. Louis.

A Cargo Route

The Mississippi has been a cargo route for more than 200 years. Large boats began carrying **lumber**, cotton, and other goods up and down the river in the 1800s. Today, about 500 million tons (455 t) of cargo are carried by Mississippi barges each year.

◀ Mississippi steamboats were once a common sight on the river. Today, replica boats like this are used for tourist cruises.

Steamboats and Barges

In early times, Native American trappers used canoes to carry furs to trading posts along the river. Later, steamboats were used on the river. With their powerful engines, steamboats could travel against the current more easily. This meant that they could carry goods and passengers the length of the river.

Today, fleets of barges travel the Mississippi. Carrying goods by barge is environmentally friendly and a cost-effective method. A single barge can carry 1,655 tons (1,500 t) of cargo. It would take 15 railway wagons or 58 trucks to transport the same load.

The Steamboat Era

In 1811, the first Mississippi steamboat, the New Orleans, traveled from Pittsburgh to New Orleans to test the waters for navigation. By 1860, more than 1,000 steamboats were on the river. The steamboat boom brought prosperity to many cities. But within a few years, the arrival of the railways brought the steamboat age to an end.

▼ Tough, diesel-engined tugboats have replaced steamboats on the river.

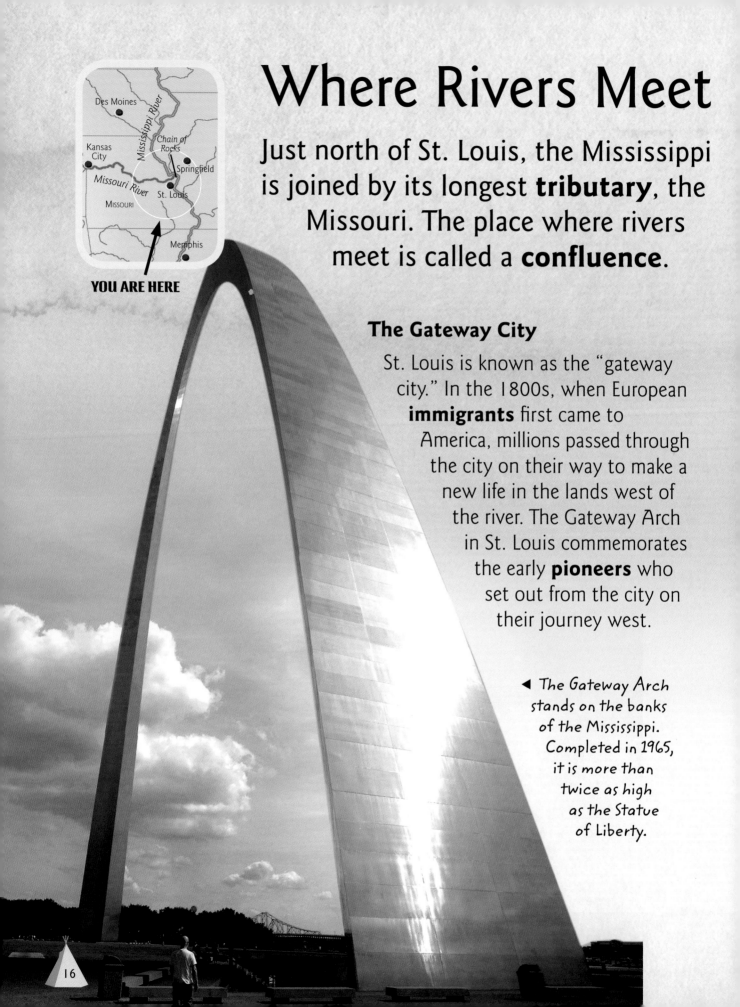

Where Rivers Meet

Just north of St. Louis, the Mississippi is joined by its longest **tributary**, the Missouri. The place where rivers meet is called a **confluence**.

YOU ARE HERE

The Gateway City

St. Louis is known as the "gateway city." In the 1800s, when European **immigrants** first came to America, millions passed through the city on their way to make a new life in the lands west of the river. The Gateway Arch in St. Louis commemorates the early **pioneers** who set out from the city on their journey west.

◀ The Gateway Arch stands on the banks of the Mississippi. Completed in 1965, it is more than twice as high as the Statue of Liberty.

◀ South of the Mississippi–Missouri confluence, this canal was built to allow river traffic to bypass the Chain of Rocks rapids (below).

A Trading Hub

Because it lies close to the meeting point of two rivers, St. Louis has always been an important transport and trading point. In the early days, pioneers stopped here to buy equipment and supplies before making the long **trek** west. Later, steamboats boosted trade on the river, and the city grew into a major port.

St. Louis Today

Today, the St. Louis area is home to more than 2.8 million people. The port is still one of its busiest areas, stretching for 19 miles (30 km) on either side of the river. The port contains more than 100 piers, **wharves**, and docks. It also has 55 fleeting areas where barges wait for towboats to take them downriver.

The Chain of Rocks

After meeting the Missouri, the Mississippi sweeps round in a 17-mile (27-km) curve known as the Chain of Rocks. The rapids were so dangerous for boats that a canal was built in 1940 to bypass them. The canal stretches 8.4 miles (13.5 km), rejoining the Mississippi just north of downtown St. Louis.

The Missouri

YOU ARE HERE

At St. Louis, you make a detour to explore the Missouri River. Although the Missouri is a tributary of the Mississippi, it is the longest river in North America.

▼ The Missouri River flows through the Rocky Mountains of northern Montana.

The Rocky Mountains

The Missouri starts its journey in the Rocky Mountains of Montana. It tumbles over rapids and waterfalls, cutting deep **gorges** through the rock. Later, it reaches the flatter lands of the Great Plains and widens out into a series of lakes. This is the corn and cattle country of the Midwest.

▶ The Missouri is sometimes known as the Big Muddy because of the rich, brown sediment that colors its waters.

The Great Plains

Before the arrival of European **settlers**, the Great Plains were home to more than a million Native Americans. Tribes such as the Blackfoot, Lakota, and Cheyenne lived here in tents called **tepees**. They moved from place to place, following the huge herds of bison that roamed the prairie.

From the 1800s onward, the Plains tribes were steadily hunted down and driven off their lands by white settlers.

Wheat Country

For a century or more, the Great Plains were intensively farmed. Today, the region is still the main source of wheat for the United States, but many farmers are leaving it. As people drift away to the towns, the prairies are once again being turned over to buffalo herds.

▶ Bison gave Native Americans meat, skins for clothing and shelter, and bones to make tools.

Missouri Mud

As the Missouri flows south, it carries sediment made of mud and stones down from the mountains. When the river floods, the sediment, or silt, is left behind on the floodplain. In the past, the silt created rich farmland. Today, much of it ends up trapped behind giant dams farther upstream.

Missouri River
Illinois
Springfield
St. Louis
Ohio River
Missouri
Tennessee
Mississippi River
Memphis
YOU ARE HERE

Flood Alert!

Back on the Mississippi, you reach the lower river. Heavy spring rains and quickly melting snow can cause devastating floods in this area.

▼ *Tennessee residents paddle a boat through a flooded neighborhood in May 2011.*

The floodwaters are often brought to the river by its tributaries, the Ohio and Missouri Rivers. The river basin soaks up some of the water. But if the soil becomes **saturated**, the water rushes down the tributaries to the main stream, which bursts its banks and floods the land.

◀ This barrier, known as the Morganza Spillway, can be opened to divert water from the Mississippi when the river is flooded. The spillway allows the floodwater to flow safely out into the Gulf of Mexico.

A Great Flood

Between April and May 2011, huge storms dumped record rainfall on the Mississippi basin, causing some of the biggest floods in nearly 100 years. Crops and **livestock** were destroyed. Many people had to leave their homes when floodwaters were diverted to protect the cities of New Orleans and Baton Rouge.

Levees

Along the banks of the Mississippi, sloping walls called **levees** (right) have been built to keep the river from overflowing. The levees reduce the impact of floods, but they do not remove the danger completely.

Levees

Levees help to prevent flooding by containing the flow of a river within low mounds or embankments. Because levees tend to make a river flow faster, they can make flooding more likely at other points of the river. For this reason, once one levee is built, others have to be built at all low points of the river system.

Cotton Country

After meeting the Ohio River, the Mississippi slows and widens. The rich soils and warm, wet climate make this area ideal for growing cotton.

Memphis

In the nineteenth century, the city of Memphis was a center of the cotton trade. Its great advantage was its location on the Mississippi River. This made it easy to transport cotton to Europe, and to the northern and eastern United States. Memphis became so famous as a cotton town that it was known as "King Cotton."

▼ Farmers harvest cotton with a combine harvester. The seed heads that contain the cotton (inset) are stripped from the stems, which are thrown away.

cotton fiber

seed head

stem

◀ Memphis stands on a high **bluff** overlooking the Mississippi. The city's raised position helps to protect it from flooding.

Cotton Plantations

In the early days, cotton was picked by hand by African **slaves**. Many lived and worked on large plantations. They endured terrible hardships and many were brutally treated by white overseers. Long after slavery was abolished, black people in the southern states suffered **discrimination** and abuse. Even today, some black communities in the South are among the poorest in the United States.

The Effects of Slavery

Slavery in the southern states lasted from the sixteenth to the nineteenth century, but its effects are still felt in America today. Millions of black Americans are descended from African slaves who worked in the cotton fields. The racism that allowed slavery to flourish is still alive in many parts of the American South.

▶ Slaves worked long days in the hot sun with no breaks and without pay. This photograph from the 1860s shows a slave family in the cottonfields of Savannah, Georgia.

YOU ARE HERE

Heading South

South of Memphis, cottonfields once stretched as far as the eye could see. Today, there are new industries along the river.

▼ Giant oil **refineries** and storage depots line the river at Baton Rouge, Louisiana, (see opposite). The city also has large sugar refineries and paper mills.

Oil and Gas

When the cotton industry declined, the southern states of Arkansas, Tennessee, and Louisiana became the poorest in America. In the 1960s, when oil and natural gas were discovered, large companies such as Exxon and Gulf Oil began drilling in the region.

Since then, many industries have moved into the area. As well as car makers such as General Motors and Toyota, more than 4,000 companies provide services to the oil industry.

Baton Rouge

Baton Rouge is the capital of Louisiana and about 380 miles (610 km) downriver from Memphis. Until the 1950s, Baton Rouge was a small port. When the river was widened and deepened, it could be used by oil tankers. As the oil companies explored the offshore oilfields in the Gulf of Mexico, Baton Rouge became one of the biggest U.S. ports.

Today, the river between Baton Rouge and New Orleans is lined with industrial plants. Because of pollution leaks and the haze of industrial **fumes** that hangs over it, the area has become known as the "Chemical Corridor."

▲ A cargo boat heads downriver to the port of Baton Rouge.

The "Red Stick"

The name Baton Rouge comes from French words meaning "red stick." The red stick was a mysterious marker that was found by a French sea captain who sailed up the Mississippi in 1699. The marker stood on the first high ground along the river. It was here that Baton Rouge was founded as a small wooden fort overlooking the river.

The River Delta

YOU ARE HERE

As you reach the low-lying marshes around New Orleans, the river slows and widens to form a giant, steamy wetland. This is the Mississippi River **delta**.

▼ The Louisiana bayous were formed when the river burst its banks, flooding neighboring woodland. These tough trees are mangroves.

The Bayous

At the tip of the delta, a long strip of marshy land stretches out into the sea. On either side, the swampy backwaters are known as the Louisiana bayous. These are a rich **habitat** for alligators, raccoons, otters, muskrats, and black bears. The swamps also provide a **haven** for thousands of migrating wild ducks from the north.

◀ These delta wetlands are a rich habitat for wildlife. They also provide a vital natural defense against storms and tidal waves.

The Changing River

*Because of silt buildup, the Mississippi's route to the gulf is constantly changing. Scientists predict that if flood defenses fail, the river will leave its present **course** through Baton Rouge and New Orleans and find a more direct route to the gulf via the Atchafalya River or Lake Pontchartrain.*

A Threatened Landscape

Not long ago, silt from the Mississippi added 0.4 square miles (1 sq km) of land to the delta every two years. Today, saltwater is invading the swamps, forcing out freshwater fish and slowly eroding the coastline.

Another threat is pollution from oil spills. One of the worst was the Deepwater Horizon spill in 2010. Oil from below the seabed poured ashore following an explosion on a British Petroleum (BP) oil rig. Millions of fish and seabirds were **contaminated**. Local people and relief agencies are still working to repair the damage to the environment and the local economy.

▼ Mississippi alligators were once hunted for their skin. Today, they are a protected species.

YOU ARE HERE

New Orleans

Your journey ends with a visit to New Orleans. This amazing city has survived floods, wars, and tropical storms to become a melting pot of people and cultures from all over the world.

▼ *New Orleans is known as the "Crescent City" because of its location on a bend of the Mississippi.*

New Orleans was the first town built on the Mississippi and is the river delta's most important city. It became a settlement because it lay at the mouth of the river and controlled the only trade route into the country. Most of the city lies below the river's flood level.

levee

◀ Floodwalls and drainage channels are vital to protect New Orleans from flooding. This levee was rebuilt and strengthened following Hurricane Katrina.

Hurricane Katrina

Because New Orleans is low-lying, it is very vulnerable to flooding. In August 2005, a powerful tropical storm swept across the Gulf of Mexico, creating a huge tide of water that overwhelmed the city's flood defenses. A total of 1,863 people died in the disaster, making it one of the worst in U.S. history.

Today, New Orleans is a busy port and an important cultural and tourist center, but it also struggles with high unemployment, poverty, and crime. Many people are still trying to rebuild their lives after the floods that struck the city in the wake of **Hurricane** Katrina in 2005.

Customs and Cultures

During its history, many different peoples settled in New Orleans. This mixture of cultures gives it a unique atmosphere. It is now home to 1.2 million people, including African-Americans and groups descended from early French and Spanish settlers known as Creoles.

▶ A street performer plays jazz on the Mississippi waterfront.

Glossary

bluff a steep hill or cliff overlooking a river

channel the shape formed by the banks and bed of a river

confluence a meeting of two rivers

contaminate to spoil, damage, or poison

course the route followed by a river

delta an area of marshy land where a river flows out to sea

discrimination unfair treatment

divert to steer or channel away from

dredger a boat used to scoop sediment from the bed of a river

fertile good for growing

floodplain the area affected by a river's floodwaters

fume harmful gas or vapor

glacier a slow-moving mass of ice

gorge a steep, rocky river valley

habitat the natural home of a plant or animal

harvest to gather or collect a crop

haven a safe place

hazard a danger or obstacle

hurricane a violent tropical storm

hydroelectric energy generated by flowing water

immigrant a person who moves to another country to start a new life

irrigating piping or pumping water to a field

levee a sloping wall or bank built to prevent flooding

livestock farm animals such as cows or sheep

lumber felled trees

mammal an animal that gives milk to feed its young

migrate to move from one place to another

pioneer someone who sets out to make a new life in unknown or dangerous territory

prairie flat or gently rolling grassland found in North America

raccoon furry mammal found in North America

refineries places where oil is processed

reservation an area of land that is set aside for Native Americans

reservoir an artificial lake in which water is stored

saturated full of water

sediment broken-down rocks and stones carried downstream by a river

settler a person who builds a home in new surroundings (see also **pioneer**)

silt fine sediment carried downstream by a river

slave a person who is owned by another and forced to work without pay

source the place where a river begins

stern wheel the rotating paddle attached to the back of a boat

talon the sharp claws of a bird or animal

tepee a traditional Native American tent

trek a long or difficult overland journey

tributary a stream or river that flows into another, larger stream or river

waterwheel a wooden wheel turned by a stream or river

wharf (*pl*. **wharves**) a place beside a river where goods are unloaded

Mississippi Quiz

Look up information in this book or online. Find the answers on page 32.

1 Match the captions to the pictures.

1

2

3

4

5

6

A A Mississippi tugboat

B A raccoon

C A mangrove tree

D A Native American tepee

E A waterwheel

F An oil rig

2 These places can all be found along the Mississippi. Place them in order, starting with the ones furthest from the Gulf of Mexico:

Memphis
Minneapolis
Baton Rouge
New Orleans
St. Louis
Lake Itasca

3 True or false?

The Mississippi is the longest river in the United States.

4 Mississippi trappers hunted this animal for its fur. What is it?

Websites and Further Reading

Websites

- *www.riverworksdiscovery.org*
  Lively and informative site exploring America's waterways

- *www.nps.gov/miss/forkids/index.htm*
  Fun facts and activities about the Mississippi

- *http://discovery.mnhs.org/forestfieldsfalls/*
  Interactive site exploring the history of Minneapolis and its people

Further Reading

Adil, Janeen R. *Mississippi River* (Wonders of the World). Weigl, 2013.

Marsico, Katie. *The Mississippi River* (Social Studies Explorer). Cherry Lake Pub., 2013.

Simon, Charnan. *The Mighty Mississippi* (Geography of the World). The Child's World, Inc., 2014.

Index

Answers to Mississippi Quiz

1 1D, 2B, 3A, 4C, 5F, 6E. **2** Lake Itasca, Minneapolis, St. Louis, Memphis, Baton Rouge, New Orleans. **3** False. The Missouri is longer. **4** A North American beaver.